Now | Flourish | Northern | Cardinal

Small Harbor Publishing

Cover art: Laura Page, "Cardinal"
Cover design: Brianna Protesto
Interior design: Claire Eder
Editor: Beth Bolton
Publisher: Allison Blevins
Director: Kristiane Weeks-Rogers
Managing Editor: Bianca Dagostino

NOW | FLOURISH | NORTHERN | CARDINAL
DARREN C. DEMARREE
ISBN 978-1-957248-57-8
Harbor Editions,
an imprint of Small Harbor Publishing

Now | Flourish | Northern | Cardinal

Selected Poems: 2005–2025

Darren C. Demaree

Harbor Editions
Small Harbor Publishing

Contents

Now | Flourish | Northern | Cardinal

Ohio #5

The sun is up. The sun is gone.
The red barn is still there,

chasing what moves towards it.
Too much of the what is spent

on the silhouette of its coming.
A religion for any moment, I believe

in nothing—I believe in Ohio.
How glad I am to be so simple

as to write love poems for a state
shaped like a swollen heart.

We Did Our Best to Breathe Into It

Lung punctured; we did our best to breathe
into the sheep's mouth, Emily even covered
the bloody hole from where the metal—shorn
from the fence post first stuck the animal—
stuck deep into the soft, red tissue, now unwilling
to expand the way it should. We did too much
for an animal we witnessed get injured from our car;
did too much to bloody our clothes on Route 3,
while family waited for us to eat a holiday meal,
but we needed to save something then, needed
to put our mouths on something desperate,
fighting to survive with righteous intention. We,
yelling about sex—the having it, the not having it
enough—saw the spearing take the shoulder first,
then plunge deeper still, while Emily took the gravel
quickly and we burst from the car in shock.
The animal died before the farmer, the owner,
or the veterinarian could arrive, or pronounce hope
& I, with my tongue warm from the expellant
of life, looked at my lovely wife, her sweater torn;
& I with my tongue, my tears only for the sheep,
asked her to hold me, despite my wavering hands.

The Tension Between the Concrete and the Ethereal

Sank the dark, the lines
we've drawn in the air,
the yellow of which

appears only in fading.
Breathless, because more breath
only pushes the printless beach

closer to the dirty echo
we've constructed below.
Heaven or no, who can speak

for anyone? I've climbed
stairs to reach metal cans;
I've fallen down freeing a bird.

"What the Fuck Are You Telling Me?"
—Ray Mancini, the night after the fight

Roasting guilt, heaped
like coals no one wanted
to carry, they told Mancini
the kid was in pretty bad
shape. They told him the kid
was dying; they told him
his brain was already dead;
they told him about the 14th
round being seconds too
long for the kid. Ray was
alive, pulped, some of him
left in pieces still on the ring
next to the already fading
opponent he feared more
than any other, because he
knew the kid was going to
come without any end.
"What the fuck are you telling
me?" Ray, I'm telling you
that was no bull you put down,
but the kid was going to keep
at you until the stretcher
had a body to carry. The kid
was a fucking man, intent
on doubling your intent
to win, in the dark if necessary—
& even though I keep looking,
I can find no blame for you.

How Vital Sport?

It has to be
                something.
The poverty, the many
fathers
& miles of family held
        up by canvas,
canvassed by the other
bloke. I think the whole
worlds
of the fighters should stand
in the corner with them,
teacher, trainer, mother,
        & the spectacle
should be forced to fit
        inside the bucket
of humanity—what's left
of it. It has to be something
more than what it looks like,
or we have taken
                warriors,
men
who could be great
men
        if they lived
long enough;   men
led around like horses,
        beaten like horses,
buried like soldiers
                with no flag.

Firework Over the Retention Pond #1

Be coming home,
the spectacle of it,
the moral inaccuracy

of the realm of light
in the context of couch
covers, the great salvation

of hiding the depth
of our leavings. Crumb
of my past, you taste

of manic silence,
& my father's voice
washes out of nothing.

Firework Over the Retention Pond #4

We spent our summer
around the water; we walked
city blocks around the water,

waiting for lights
that could make it over
our heads, our reflections

limited severely by our heights
& the eager moon,
that always had us colliding

into eager transitions, balked.
If we had been from a larger town,
we would have tried making love.

We Are Arrows #2

The sheets are warmth.
     We are lithe, we are
not busted in presentation.
     If in retrospect, you
saw us diving in flight, it was
the wind shaking us, as we
are not with the wind.
     We are arrows that
began with the muscles of a
uniquely driven animal that
lives four stories in four
realities at all times.
     The sheets are
warmth the same way the
desert is warmth.   It is
not cruel for us to find the
shoulder blades of this world,
and plunge through to
another world—in fact we talk
about leaving our bodies to
do this all of the time.

We Are Arrows #8

Vulnerable without
action, we have lost
too much blood to
vibrate only in the
marrow.   Offered
as an integral piece;
offered as a toy, we
have thrust both feet
into the mouth of the
ground, lit the small
fat in our bottom lip
on fire, and recited
our demands like
they are prayers to
a flush desert.
So full of chances
to tongue the eyes
of every photograph,
of every combustion,
of every lover—we
hinge each grain
against another grain,
and as the wave
develops we learn
again how shakable
a singular flower can
be.   Sign of no
shadow, we are never
lonely; we are direct
in our belief that the
sun above us is
waiting for a good
dance to frame
the next mountain.

We Are Arrows #26

Locked into the black bear
thrashing against the flow of
the river, I took one picture of
his empty paws; I took one
picture of his desire to
consume any fish willing to
leave the water; I took one
picture of our campsite after
he destroyed it.
Fruitless, a garnered
lacking, I have never cared
more about nature than I did
after he took a swipe at the
car we were hiding in. I
wanted to be that bear.
          We all wanted to be
that bear.   If we,
in failure, had the strength to
turn the countryside into the
littering of our tantrums, our
real fights would last only one
fishing trip, and our hearts
would be tremendous with
such unruly strength.

We Are Arrows #88

Isolated, we could be a
violent bird.
        Flocked, we could be
violent birds.   The panic that
follows our descent—our path
to be buried in shoulder, in
hamstring, in the bloom of
the crops—that is as
predictable as gravity.
        Isolated, it looks for a
moment, like we could be
scratching at the sun.
        Flocked, it looks for a
moment, like we could be in
tandem with nature, the
revolution that only nature
can bring, but just as we were
all burned into being, the
cooling happens as our target
chooses us from the ground.

We Are Arrows #209

Our gladness, as small as
sugar, lifts the suspect of our
control over our own hearts,
puts the blood pump into our
own hands, and slows it to wait
for our own chosen sparks.
                    We are
animals all day—denial of our
small pleasures can lead to
irrational discontent.

     Our gladness, as small
as sugar, as soon as now, can
be a crutch without the
weight to place on top of it,
but that is why we have
moved past dragging our
bellies in the sand.

All the Birds Are Leaving #60

It's one growth
from the grove
of the ear, an echo

that gives eyes
to time, and teaches it
that though the tree

becomes the sky,
surrendering
to the canvas

unlimited, the tree
still holds the song
of our first attention.

We strain, always,
for a message
from the stars

& though the birds
appear headed
that direction,

we should consider
first where they
make their home,

where their voice
first reached past
the root system.

Flush to the oak—
if you hear anything
it is the truth.

All the Birds Are Leaving #64

There are animals
that keep treasure

in their bellies
& though some of us,

our old leaders,
looked as if they did,

too, we are judged
rarely for what we can

swallow. Thin-
throated, our counting

of time isn't keeping
time—it's naming it

before we even know
what it is. I remember

etc., is our best
closeness to thick

reality. The sinew
we will never see,

but we have infinite
names for that, too.

All the Birds Are Leaving #79

I am learning
more

not to compare
anything

to fruit,
especially time

which arrived
before us,

ripe
& arrived

ready to leave
the vine—

almost an oil
already,

we were born
mid-flight

in a bath
of spoil;

but that's why
I am learning

to love
everything,

even as it turns
into the smell
of having been.

Emily as a Pious Crowd & a Rabbit

Living presence, so full of leg meat
& belief in the corduroy jacket
of a more modern Jesus, we tried

to make blood sausage
from the collection of rabbits
we found and chased over the water—

simple in a boat, we never came
up with enough clean flesh
to ferry ourselves back to shore

& I forget if we ever tried the bread
& I forget if we ever tried the fish
& I know, even lost, we ate well.

Emily as a Leveling of the Ground

Across the snow,
the sea change of Ohio,
the axe splits wood

as an empty threat
to the whole world—
but then again, hands

can motion the life
right out of this thing.
Personally involved

in the end of the world,
what the living do
is command the rags

& muscles to be easy
with pleasure;
to take the blanket

& pull it over all heads;
to kick legs
like an ornery child—

a knowing child
with a flat surface
to give in to an eyelid.

I found Emily;
that means I am ready
for the rest of you

to close your eyes.

Emily as the Length of a Fox

I haven't the time
to find a bluff
to overlook an expanse
& understand
Emily.
I am in the densest part
of the woods with her
now, the deep
where you touch
everything at once
& believe in the small
bits of your flesh
that you can predict
the next tree that will move
& the next animal
that will eat the next animal
& that shared breath
of meat
is as indelicate
as closeness can be.

Emily As A Smile Would Have Ruined the Picture

There was one look, one picture
of Emily in a bathtub right before
we got married—she was travelling

with her family; she was in Madrid
or Paris or Istanbul, and she had been gone
for a couple of weeks, so I had been

drunk for a couple of weeks
& she knew that I had been drunk
for a couple of weeks, so she sent me

a picture of her in the bathtub, one
breast covered, hair in a way I'd never
seen before, looking directly at the faucet

& so surely the tatters of my world
collected into a whole woman
so beautiful that when I got the picture

I accidently deleted the picture.
I remember it clearly though: her face,
elegant, angry that she didn't have

her hands wrapped around the back
of my head to pull me off of the bottle.
She wanted to bury me in her beauty

& that almost worked too well.
I am sober. I don't have that picture.
I have Emily. She looks at me now.

Emily as a Puma Crosses

A day without the tan
rags of Ohio,
I saw Emily walk naked

across our front lawn.
She was drunk, aware
that we can't have drunks

in our house anymore
& without a single tear
or regret for her state,

she stalked our home,
moving faster, smoother,
without a look to the neighbors

that were lining up to see
the last bit of her girlishness
be swallowed up by time

& her inebriation. It takes
an hour for each drink
to vanish from our system

& at dawn, Emily knocked
on the door, still naked,
still a mother of two,

yet somehow more dangerous
than she had been before.
She napped all day. I didn't want

to shake her, for what if
she was still dreaming as a girl,
as a puma, without fear.

Emily as the Audacity of the Red Egg

for Sam Roxas-Chua

The sun is never white.
The chest collects
only breakable bones.
Each new day
carries with it a tribe
so native to this
moment the wars
do not have the time
to fill our throats
with a second cry.
I look to focus my eyes
on the landscape
& the fog that once
hugged Ohio charges
me. I relax my gaze
& I see Emily
as a red egg, paused
on the impossible tip
of love. I see her
in defiance of all want.
A table cannot starve.

Emily As I Hold Three of Her Shoes

I would
write poems

about swans
if I gave

a shit about
swans.

The swans
you're

thinking of—
do they

have anything
to do

with Emily?

Emily as a Book of Endings

For Leslie Harrison

I chose Emily, because I knew
that if she chose me
I could prepare for death

in a way that made my desperation
to keep living something tangible.
Now, with each child we have

I am cemented in the panic
of the living. Now, since she
keeps choosing me

every morning, I am able
to taunt mortality in a way
that will leave claw marks

in the fields of Ohio.
How glorious it will be
to be dragged from the living

& to scream one name; to spit
one name at my weakening
grip; to expect the strength

to return to me just like
the thousands of other times
I've used her name to live longer.

Emily as She Dropped the Lantern at My Feet

I always wear cotton
just in case Emily needs me
to go up in flames.

I get to be the one that holds
her fire! How tender
of her to choose me

from the crashing to burn
just enough for her to lead
our children to safety.

How terrible it must be for a man
to have less of a purpose
than to be burned like me.

Emily as Where We Sigh

I am not sad,
nor am I languishing
here with Emily—

I just needed to let go
of that air that briefly
was supporting me

until she returned.
Chest without gradient,
I am free to join us

as the hawk joins
the simple sky
with great mission.

Emily as Measureless

I know how
many hand
lengths she is.

I do not know
how to stop
measuring.

Emily as Our Lust is a Common Lust

Seriously—
it's almost all
buttons.

Nude Male with Echo #1

Inhabiting the slip
& wobble, the surge
to silence that is
the physical form
of an un-soldering
male, I have paused
all of my momentum
to stand before
anything else happens
to my layering,
& to watch every rising,
& watch again
what can happen
after that moment
has given in to the next.
I see strength
when I ready myself
to see such things.

Nude Male with Echo #55

I have tried many times to believe
that I do not exist. The pads beneath
the pads of fingertips—right where

my identification turns into synapse—
that is where my triviality ends.
This is an incredibly layered world

& I have felt most things most
of the time. When I am mirrored,
I touch the mirror; that is my problem.

Nude Male with Echo #70

I wanted to tighten the lines
so I could be supple when I chose
to be supple. I wanted to sleep
in the path of the touching
& leave the wandering to those
that could create new words for wandering,
& while they contemplated the road,
I would be the road. I was almost
trampled there. That is why
I smile almost all of the time;
there was such incredible beauty
in the almost passing and the holding on
that it dragged me to the swelling
tulip that is here—that is now.

Nude Male with Echo #197

Called vivid
& departing the rhythm
of the twisting

admittance of one body
into one landscape,
it felt like an opening—

like actual birth,
making room for me
to be shadow

& to make shadows;
& I danced
in front of you from

a great distance
& that, for unknown
reasons, gave you

a hope made famous
by your return
to the unsubtle steps.

Nude Male with Echo #244

When I sleep in the garage
on the broken hammock
near the broken lawn mowers

& the decorative tools—too old
to be used anymore, too rusty
to be sold anymore—I feel each

wind that works through the block
cement walls. It's a cold tickle,
but I never shiver near so much

metal. There is a beauty
in the resistance that all of us have
refused to be thrown out

for good. I nap there, beneath
the campaign sign from my father's
city council run, because when

I open my eyes I see my favorite
shade of blue catching the sun
before it reaches my aching body

& I remember that my name
will be said, even in defeat,
if I declare myself a candidate.

Nude Male with Echo #257

It doesn't matter
that the edges are sharp.
You are cut on entry.
You are cut in transition.
You are cut into pieces
when you exit.
One dove bleeds on our faces
& that doesn't matter
either. We are born
with adrenaline
& that means we will
be allowed to play God
in a few scenes. So,
all of the roles are ours.
The landscape chooses
a costume for us
before each day opens
& that is the best
I can explain waking.

Nude Male with Echo #299

Suddenly moonlight
& we are befuddled
in the pause

of the ghost
which cannot touch us.
It is night.

That doesn't matter.
We were talking
about how it was pretty

grand that we are
both oils, rubbed
against each other,

never combining,
never leaving the scene—
just sliding

in the punch of hope
& never, ever finding
a balance

that gives us more
pause than the moon
at variable times.

Nude Male with Echo #319

Hit the dead
colors, the white without
& the static black.

Let the rush of red
find the brim
& let it shake the god

damn episodic people
that move from room
to room without

ever running away from
or towards anything
other than an opening.

The museums
are so fucking cold
because of these people.

Decorating the Phrase

Every word
shares two skins
with the tongue

that releases it
into the world,
& Sam Cooke

could lift
& separate
the same word

fifteen times
in a row
& you would

still believe
there was a soul
in the repetition.

Saying "I Love You" Fifteen Times in a Row

There is no peace
in the fattening up
of one's emotional

declarations. Those
words can become
the weight only

& possessing no bones
smother to smother
to smother the ears

in a desire the heart
can never register.
Love becomes dark matter

if it appears to have
no beginning
& no hope of ending.

Ten Grand

There was a price
to get each woman
to stay out of court,

to stay out of the papers,
to stay five hundred feet
away from Sam Cooke,

& that price of doing
business was factored in
& deducted with each

new set of papers
from the judge. Sam
had the money

& ten grand—that was
enough to buy
some silence from

their seething.
As long as Bumps
wrote those checks

& intercepted that mail,
the man could sing
& believe

he was Sam Cooke
& that was enough
truth for his smile.

He Was Wearing an Overcoat, One Shoe, and Nothing Else

Love was the wrong word,
but even the bullets wanted
their way with Sam Cooke.

In 1965, Bobby Womack Was an Asshole, but It Wasn't Really His Fault

To be twenty
& in love with the wrong woman—
a widowed woman

who dresses you up
in her dead husband's clothes
& makes you sing his songs

& collides with your body
like an atom that must be split
to save the whole world

she's constructed
for the two of you to play in—
that is a motion

that makes a young man
tuck his arms behind his back
& allow whatever may come.

Barbara made him a faithful
version of Sam Cooke
& that must have been pleasant

for her. Still, Bobby,
when you told the press
that his kids were calling

you "Daddy,"
dammit man, you should
have known better.

When Men Talk About Sam Cooke

The slant is freezing
& the silence that follows
after the songs stop

playing—after we hear
just how prideful he was
& important during

the movement's first progress
of the sixties—what comes
next is always nothing;

they've fleshed him out
just enough to be shot
with great mystery.

Nickel to a dollar, those
men will name the women
Sam Cooke mounted

as a flap of character,
as an ornery way to clap
him on the back

for being Sam Cooke
& I, to join the chorus,
first made a list of the women

he ruined during the process—
how they struggled, how
they died to leave

those children behind
with their own parents.
He tortured these women

with short visits
& tremendous promises
& that voice they could always

hear on the radio—so powerful,
so soothing—but two and a half
minutes was all he was good for.

Sweet Wolf #1

We've named all of the animals
& we've put our fingers into the names
of each of them. We've dragged

their names up to our faces
& forced them to meet our made-
up world. Sometimes we are given

kisses. Sometimes there is
a great warmth. We know they
are wild. We know there is danger.

We know if we allow the sweet wolf
into our veins it will become
the alpha inside our own bodies

& yet, what a pool to drown in.
The chemicals of each breed
brings a new threat.

There have been so many Ohioans
eaten from the inside out
that I've been forced

to re-think exactly what these drugs
are in our world. They are wolves.
We've been raised by them.

Sweet Wolf #13

Lost in the acreage,
sin can stretch out a bit;
can sing the crowd

into a burning skeleton;
can make a path
out of the ashes

of each field party,
& when the sun becomes
a witness, how many

stray animals do you
think it will count?
How many sheriffs

are found sleeping
in their off-duty trucks?
It's useless to govern

most of Ohio, when most
of Ohio is smoke, is anti-
treasure, is empty alarm.

Monroe Mills, Ohio

The mercy
of the lord
is for the dead

& since we
hold so many
of our dead

without re-
membering
why they died,

the mercy
of the lord
is only

for the dead.
Nobody tosses
out the drugs

of the dead.
That's not how
this works.

Utica, Ohio

There is a metaphysical assumption
that transcendence begins in the mind
& I have risen many times

that way, but in Central Ohio
it takes a little extra to be lifted
above the diamond cutters

& small-town politicians
that you know were forced
to leave the church deacons

because they were watching girls
change in the basketball locker room.
It takes good, hard drugs

to believe that you have the ability
to range into a naturalness
that feels as large as the world,

& I find no fault in those that take
drugs to escape, but I miss
so many people

that never came back to me.

Ode to the Corner of the Drug House Down the Gravel Road off the Two-Lane Highway #29

Hardened in the air,
my mouth has gone
thin with the season,

which is no longer fall,
no longer winter—
this season is Ohio;

this season is the drug
season. The body
count is the same

as what it would take
to remove the context
of the stars in the sky.

Ode to the Corner of the Drug House Down the Gravel Road off the Two-Lane Highway #60

The eye of the haven
from the outside
looks like a slit—

an uneager wound
in a terrible house—
& from the back

of this car I can feel
no prelude; I can see
no future. That

corner never knew
me sober.
I feel loss

will find me
once this shit
wears off—

& then what will
I get to look out of?
I used to see all

of Ohio through
that damage.
I could smell

the water from
the retention pond
turning against me.

The Field Party #1

in the feeder of ohio the fires burn with bodies as well as they burn with the furniture that once held the bodies it doesn't matter if it's summer & you can feel the heat from the two-lane the fires will be lit all night long we raise our children to track those gatherings to bring the drinks to those gatherings to bring the cord and the blood in the cord to not fear becoming part of that fire to know that the fire is ohio to laugh in spite of ohio as it masquerades as fate and then becomes fate in a twist once it has you on the bench by the fire staring at the fire feeding fall with the fire knowing that there will be no crisp without the fire without your body without your willingness to see at night far past the rational hours the midwest always claims to be all the hours

A Letter to Auguste Rodin, Explaining the Bombing of the Thinker

The pedestal is just fine,
but your son, dear sir,
has lost his legs

& yes, we've come up
with reasons why
somebody placed dynamite

like flowers at your grave.
We know there can be
no comfort for a dead man

about a cloned son
that never actually lived,
but this felt like the right

thing to do under such
circumstances. We've
decided not to heal him.

He will remain un-alive.
He will be placed back on
his pedestal, without repair.

A Damaged Thinker #16

Like every man who has seen fire
erupt from a metal casing, I believe
limits are the exotic animals

of this world. We know them
because we mourned their passing
slightly before we swung, unloved

by the expired limitations, the color
of feather we can now only paint;
like we must create, again, a life

from the intended view of modern
memory, the fire that finds us,
our face, after it takes our legs—

that was an animal, too, a live one.

A Damaged Thinker #20

Drive the moon
down, past knowledge
& beneath the cables

sewn up from the orchards
I've never seen, where
the artists make

their deals; where they
long to tease the diamond
tethers that dance

the firmament, gather
the beauty into the essence
of silence. I heard none

of the explosion, because I was
too taken by a neck that won't
move. I fell face-first. I felt

cheated by the placement
of the dynamite. If I fell back,
I could have had the sky.

A Letter to Auguste Rodin About Useless Wine

We've been mud
& bird

& dealt with
terrible loneliness

& we needed
a red that could

action us against
our own red,

but after you died
& he lost his legs,

the idea that we
needed

to be softened,
become swamp

again, was left
wanting

more bronze;
more marble.

An Acceptance of Art

Show the whites
of your eyes
to be a lumbering
pair—not searching,
but searched for
& given, awarded
forever by the feather
of costume bird's
maker. I am willing
to be lied to. I am
desperate for it.

blue and blue and blue #3

there is language
in every silence

blue and blue and blue #6

i was
born far
enough

away
that i
believed

you had
control
of your

tongue;
how ugly
it slaps

against
& over
the tide

while i
attempt
to dream

of hold-
ing
anything

at all

blue and blue and blue #63

hold the almonds
in your fist
& when you've lost

all of them,
say a prayer to
the ocean's bottom

& make a promise
to lose the rest
of your fist as well

blue and blue and blue #133

the sea has come
to harvest me
& that is a religion

for any moment
& that is exactly
why i have removed

my jacket, shown
my circus skin
to the moon's eye—

that is why
i am quiet when
my name is called

blue and blue and blue #134

a good wave
knocks every pill
out of your pocket

Unfinished Murder Ballad: The Only Dedicated Cowboy in Columbus, Ohio Objects to the Price of His Black Coffee

Slenderness worn from where muscle once wanted to grow, then grew only to fit the active frame and casting of a man who had no room in his world for the modernity of the city he lived in—he knew that if he was going to have the energy to make it through his day as a chew-spitting communications technician at AT&T, he would need a lunch time coffee. Up at dawn, he had tended to his crop on the fire escape, he had fed all the animals before he fed himself, and all three of his cats appreciated that sort of man. Now, though, the slack before him was demanding two dollars for a black coffee, and that wore on him the way a bad hand would have worn on the Duke. His father had been a tax attorney and bequeathed him no rifle. He would need to go to the pawn shop again.

Unfinished Murder Ballad: The Walls Slid Back Down, Joining

She had no time to describe the lost things, but the trail was epic, so we chased, first, where she was coming from. There was the dead, and that was expected. There was the blood that seemed to be dragged by her out into the woods to be killed again, and that disregard was maybe most impressive. It takes dedication to kill the killed and do so in a public way. What we couldn't see from any great distance was that she had demolished her parent's house as well. She didn't set any fires. She took it apart piece by piece, smashing the strong bits, being gentle where she could. It looked like a puzzle violently undone. It looked bathed in her parent's remains. She must have been working on it for months.

Unfinished Murder Ballad: The Sea Naked

She wanted the desert. She wanted to shiver only at night. The fear she brought with her, to camp under so many heavenly witnesses. He fought back, baggy with the tequila she bought. He fought back wide, and not once did he strike her face. The three seconds between the bruising and the grand leak must have looked like a celebration of good bodies from so far away, must have reminded the fathers of what the sling-shot motion can do when enough explosions take place close to the heart of all sky. At least, for a little while, it must have resembled a creation tale.

Unfinished Murder Ballad: The Girl Was a Raspberry

Killing a mile of steam at a time, the fog pouring like the best lies that can trace the valley with a plastic bag tenderness, and that girl, I tell you, she was a raspberry. She said she had real skin, but the world around her could only be swallowed, never chewed without leaving moments of terror around the mouths of all the boys she called to. I know her fatalities talked more without the days counting them, and I also know her tight intentions could be like seeds beginning to grow underneath a molar. No man had straight teeth after he met her. Part of that was because they were valley people. Part of that was that she wouldn't lay down with any of them without a large tree branch within her thick arm's reach.

Unfinished Murder Ballad: Caribou

Rush the darkness. Bend your head down. Allow your crown to plunge through the urgency of the now. If there really was a person there, will it ever matter to you? It should, but then again it isn't always about should. There are whole nations un-buried. They were faithful, intent on good, and it took only one ambition to render their poignancy moot. Sometimes you are in a forest of people. Sometimes those people carry no seed.

Shari's Lemon Sour Cream Blueberry Pie

for Shaindel Beers

A simple plant
doesn't necessarily hold
a simple bloom. Joy

can redefine you
if it's messy enough.
Sing without comprehension!

Not all crusts can carry
their own vernacular
to the dinner table,

but when that happens,
when our tongues
get good & sloppy

by attempting to taste
every syllable, that counts
as a love language.

You don't have
to be able to repeat it
to make it a song.

Huckleberry Pie
for Kelly Morse

Every berry
has an accent
if you give it

a chance
to speak.
Sugar can

drown almost
any identity,
but not

a huckleberry.
I've seen whole pies
propose marriage

to a County
Commissioner's niece.
I like a dessert

that pays for dinner
& then stays
at the table

just long enough
to let the crust
crumble a bit.

Mushroom Pie

for Lauren Dostal

I love trading
shadow for shadow.
I know the high

& wide of the world
wants something
more than I have,

but with a crust
unbroken
by other depths

I am likewise
in all customs.
There are places

with better shows.
I love trading
shadow for shadow.

The Moon Is Too Big to Be the Moon

Our bodies have fathers
& yet, on the clearest nights
it appears

we all had nine mothers
& a voice they ignored
in the distance.

Some midnights
have a violent clarity
& the first one

your first child survives
will churn up
the sky for many years.

Not a Leaf, Falls Like a Leaf

Let the charging
road tar be the whole route
& instead

of us using the pavement,
forcing weight
& wheel on each inch

of the modern path,
let's tell the children
that we are carried by waves

we spent years making,
that the car is lifted
towards home

or the beach. We'll preach
to them to allow
the undulations,

put both hands
outside of the car window
& cup them,

just in case we've chosen
the right day
in the right season

for them to be given
one whole hut
of nature's allowance.

layering

the children can't help / but puff out their cheeks / when the first numb
nose of fall / makes them feign to kiss the wind / back to back / like a
promise to dying flowers / matters amidst the mulch / like our neighbors
that layer plastic / over their bushes / might be able to save / us all / like
the schools might suddenly open again / or bare faces might one day /
be as beautiful as a masked face / can be when it carries / no
autobiography of death / in a drop of spittle / like the men in my
hometown / might stop threatening me / for reading poems / over the
graves / of their children / because the president has said / i should be
buried / for warning them / that all drugs are wolves / that all wolves /
are death lobbyists / are bought by death / like our president / who has
counted dead children / by the hundreds / as bricks in a wall / that will
keep us / warm this winter / when no fabric will matter / when the
layering / i have kept specifically / for my three children / will not matter
at all / because the fires will be burning / the smell will be turning / our
stomachs / all of the kissing will end / in a proper smack / of this world
/ rushing towards the boundaries / of existence / like small lips /
wishing they did not have / to be asked / to frame the words / of a
future / they don't quite believe in

[those junk plums]

i told my children those junk plums left at the bottom of the grocery bag
were not perfect when we put them in the bag but they were on sale and
good enough for a family that doesn't get many plums now that they are
mangled and losing their juice to the bottom of the thin green bag i
struggled so mightily to remove from the dispenser we are still going to
cup their mangled flesh in our hands we are still going to eat them
however inelegant that might be we are going to pour the remnants into a
tiny cup we are going to celebrate the fact that there is still fruit in this
world that won't always be the case

[that coal]

i told my children that coal was a mountain fever that men had ridden the
blood of the mountain into the valley and then flooded the valley to that
they could pick up the paychecks off the dead bodies that floated there
and those bodies that felt the rush of cool water before they expired they
were the lucky ones and that coal in america is our fourth saddest
slaughter story but for some reason very few people have had to answer
for the body count so if they want to if they really want to my children
are welcome to tell anybody that manages or owns coal to fuck right off
because language is important and i don't want them wasting those words
on anybody that doesn't deserve it

[her body]

i told my daughter her body is no narrative her body is an ocean and a moon and there is no freckle no nail no strand of hair that she is not in charge of and that means that if we do this right she will continue the proper revolution that leads to her lifting up the whole of our government in her hands and shaking them the way they so badly want to shake her and if she doesn't stop until their tongues are flags in the wind then that is her decision because i'm not raising an american or an ohioan i'm raising a girl that will become a woman and she will know her body is whatever the fuck she decides it is and any sail that any person tries to stick in her back to change her path will be burned in a pile i give her when she no longer needs me to write such things

[you should tell me now that you don't care]

i told my children you should tell me now that you don't care that you're going to be fire-starters and con-artists and painters that you will only need me for alibis so i can let you know now that i'm your man and if this is going to be my adventure to follow you and watch your synapses fire quickly all of the time fire incorrectly and beautifully all of the time then i am in don't hurt children don't steal from poor folks do not plagiarize anything ever do you hear me other than that i'm willing to do a couple of years in jail if it means you will get to dance around this universe like you've figured something out

[you might choose to read these poems]

i told my children you might choose to read these poems in the bareness
and anxiety of your young adulthood while you search for me in the
thousands and thousands of poems i have written so that i could explore
so that i could explain so that i could hide and lie about some small
terribleness and it gives me endless joy that you will find me here right
here right now as bare as you are but feeling no anxiety at all because i
am with my children in some small way in the future when i love you
even more than i already do because that's how real love works it grows
with the epic it encircles the epic until you cannot tell why or how any of
this began but you know you know you know that if there is such a thing
as a soul it exists to be buoyed by moments like this

with an empathy so fatal #7

i want the bodies in the field
to be okay i sent my children
into that field

for the party i thought might
welcome them
now i am afraid i sent them

onto a burial ground
i sent them onto a burial ground
there was nowhere else

to send them
i couldn't stand to have them
& not share them with you

with an empathy so fatal #21

we have teeth
we show them
to politicians

with an empathy so fatal #52

i can't look at this
any other way
the world can be so dry

& i was born
with water
& i have given that

water to my children
& told them
to give it away

& they did not blink
they closed their eyes
& offered it

& now i am frightened
for their safety
there is no other way

with an empathy so fatal #56

we have done
nothing
to sew

ourselves
into the lining
of this world

when this
world stands up
we will be lost

bone requires bone #46

the lemon the muscle the anti-birth that happens with each construction
of a gun the smudges left on the landscape when an abuser ends up
holding the gun of the abused the ash the ash the ash working through
our nation's hideous volcano will give us a second blanket we do not need
hell the first blanket the attention of it was too much to begin with

bone requires bone #47

the shiver grants the premise that grief is the only emotion that can't be beaten out of you that shiver always leaves that shiver doesn't know shit anger hangs on long enough to bury you swinging against the violent tide that almost always looks like a man

if there is a river #28

spot-lit and staged the edge that slides around our split-green hearts is
not the edge of our world it's the edge of our understanding how how
how freeing it would be if we disregarded that movement or if we took it
as an invitation and removed the glove from our souls if we bared
ourselves with the wind instead of against it would we fly would we fall
more slowly would we reach the bottom of existence and move forward
from that point with the fullness of an actual survivor

if there is a river #55

the antelope drinks from the river and that act is enough to build a thousand churches

I Have No Intention of Burying My Body #52

You can call it a hymn,
or whatever the fuck—
if the fox

eats one of my fingers
then finally I will get
to be a fox.

War Commentary #51

the fuck can be taken it can be given it can be held the fuck is all this is
an important question the fuck is you is an important question fuck fuck
fuck your orange belly is a chant we can rally behind we have all been
fucked before and we are here despite the constant desire of power to
fuck us again it's amazing how quickly the new power forgets how it is to
be fucked without desire to be fucked by the slow drawing of laws isn't
pleasant but i cannot imagine the fear the powerful feel right now as they
listen to all of this fuck talk masquerading as a song to rally our sore
nation against their indiscriminate fuckety fuck fucking of our idealistic
leanings which are now much more of an idealistic cry in the shower i
imagine the sight of us all in towels wrapped up in our best profanity and
parading down the capital streets has them muttering only one word over
and over and over again

Trump as a Fire Without Light #12

New sorrow, old accuracy—we all arrived outside the community center to say his name with our teeth, to let it bounce around our mouths, to have it be chewed up while it left that cave, to see it injured in the world before it was ever heard by another soul. Such a chaotic thing, his name —such a weight, a violence in image and repetition, and now we're forced to taste it. Nobody wants to taste his name, but we must if we're going to mangle it properly.

Trump as a Fire Without Light #86

I know most of Ohio wants him to make the world like most of Ohio, but I'm telling you that most of Ohio is dead. There are dead men still running on anger and racism. There are dead women kept on budgets by those angry and fearful men. We have universities, but nobody thinks about islands when they live in a land without tides. I have a dozen relatives that consider Trump a fever dream of a president. This is the first time any of them have experienced a real high. They're not handling it well. They keep threatening me. I'm not handling it well. I've been sober long enough I could help them, but I'm not there yet. I want them to have to carry this time in their lives. I want them to realize they're going to have to lie to their grandchildren about it.

Trump as a Fire Without Light #115

The word can curdle if you keep it in your mouth all of the time, if you only use the angry corners of it a bit at a time. These men in their terrible and expensive suits—they're not chewing on their own tongues, they're chewing on the word. They roll it around. They play with it. They use it the same way they use motels. When there is a good enough excuse to fuck the scene they spit it on the floor, and those that adore them see the garden unfold in that bad carpet. All I see is their fat cheeks. All I see is a partial blessing of spittle. All I can think about is that it will be up to my children to clean those floors. How will they think of us while they demolish most of what it is we've built?

Trump as a Fire Without Light #140

I spent a night refusing my bed, refusing to calm down, refusing to be taken deeper into the dark of that night, and refusing to be softened into a gold that could be melded into his crown. I woke up sleeping dogs so they could follow me as I stomped around the ravine. I woke up children so they could eat pancakes with me at 4 am. I left my wife asleep, because she'd already stayed up talking to me until after midnight. I called my father and let it ring until, dazed, he picked up the phone. I told him I wasn't a feather. I told him he was a feather on the wing of a doomed bird. He told me he loved me, and then he hung up. I spent a morning crawling around on the roof of my house. All of the people I loved were safe beneath me, but I needed the whole of winter at that point. I needed to be blanketed in snow, and when I was I could finally sleep. When my neighbors came to their cars to head to work, they shook their heads at me, and I, their collective "Ugh", welcomed the judgment. I am not right to do things such as this, but I can think of no other role for me. I am too afraid the warmth is one of his tricks, and I am too afraid to spend even one whole minute silent on the issue.

Trump as a Fire Without Light #340

The ocean is full of motherfuckers that believed they were the ocean.

Trump as a Fire Without Light #415

The stars have opened their mouths to be indelicate against the black, to chant with the wagging tongue of the absence of heaven the same phrase in every language. There is no sleep in the cosmos. There is no retreat in the cosmos. When they chant "traitor" enough to change our weather patterns, then they have a message we should listen to.

Trump as a Fire Without Light #416

It's not cold enough to be winter. I can see everything he's doing. Still, this is a blizzard, and we are all in danger. I am driving my car on clean streets as if at any moment I could drive into the living room of a neighbor. I am listening to the storm. I am not listening for direction. I am singing in the wind. I am not safe. That part doesn't matter so much, but the muscles in my body thinks it does.

Trump as a Fire Without Light #417

He cannot hover. His weight doesn't allow that. There are fifty men and two women each holding a rope that allows him to be suspended above me while I sleep. One of those men has just wrapped that rope around his neck. There are forty-nine men and two women holding a rope that keeps him inches from my face. Two or three more appear to be admiring the corpse beside them. This all ends with his body on top of mine. I am practicing holding my breath. I am learning how to expand my chest enough that when he makes his impact he will roll off of me and into the valley of that which I cannot think of anymore.

Trump as a Fire Without Light #665

I have begged the mountain to fill the valley, and the rivers to kiss the desert. That was pointless. I can carry rock. I can carry buckets of water. I have a whole life to slightly shift the gradient of the world I see. It will be so wonderful to feel my body release these fists into the wind, and then to join the wind completely—that is enough map for the rest of the beautiful intent.

america chose to drown in the desert

i have heard the orchestra of children discovering that we cage any thrust of the garden before it can become the garden that we take the clay to hold our flowers before they can take the clay to carry water to their mouths that we are all limb and muscle and lost vein and we have never had the heart for a nation that could survive the distinction between breathing and being forced to consume an unhealthy air a measured and wild sharing of the landscape we can compost sure but we compost the native beauty before we can think to name the bloom before we ever thought to ask what the bloom was already called we are staggeringly qualified to end all life on this planet because we have already pulled a nation of mountains and rivers into the desert to bum-rush the emerging children of the i cannot stop thinking about the children as they ask for their parents in a way so raw and searching that it frames the love i have for my own children as something like a funeral avoided a funeral held without bodies because all of the bodies have been separated from each other all of the bodies that once held each other cultivated distilled the purples hope can give into a perfume that rises towards the moon above the brush in a desert america chose to drown in when all america needed to do was allow each foot step to be a gift in the old way it was a gift but instead we opened our throats to meet the sun instead we looked into the eyes of children separated from their parents and called their brokenness the flood we'd been waiting for

red milk
dayton, august 4th, 2019

do not forget that every lake in ohio is manmade the salted bodies are
not ours & yet i can count the bodies in ohio that were once ours & i can
say their names because though someone stuck the anti-seeds deep in
their flesh so that he could see their flesh arranged outside this garden
they still have names each a proper glare of a name a shine that lit old
roads scoreboards first flits of our wet landscape reflected in the loving
eyes of another they still have their names the unique seasoning of their
names this this this boy gone fat with the red milk he was given as if
there were no other nutrition in this world cannot force salt into a field
that has forever rejected salt as something elemental to our existence i
can say his name too i can say the names of those that decorated his belly
with their cheap color their cheap metal their cheap hate those names are
public as public as the cost of each syllable their barrel mouths utter to
drape our landscape with any confusion at all the boy has burst already
the rocks have begun to gather to give even more graves cover i don't
know i don't know i don't know why people keep saying i don't know this
is simple the alignment of life has shifted into a common crosshairs
we've been given a terrible promise to ensure that a finger's desire is
worth more than a whole county's crop we're turning states nations
continents into violent islands we cannot escape put your hand in the
fresh water you'll need to do so upstream down here is where the pool is
full of the runoff the leaking that cannot stop until it's decided that we
are not so weak that we must have buttons to press that can detonate a
city into a new lake that holds a color we will never be able to stomach

the wind has never cared

the wind / has never cared / about the chunks / of flesh / it pushes past
/ or the framing / of that flesh as a receptacle / for the seasons / & it is
harder / in the middle / of that field party to stand / up alone / without
getting kissed / by the stones / thrown / recklessly / from the road /
wow / the accuracy / of hate / is astounding / the bullets / the bullets /
always / find a home / don't they / & as i flail / as i always flail / with
more words / than the washing off of words / i catch no peace / i dance
with no peace / i am watched by a piece of ohio / that will always / offer
me a chair / i refuse the premise / of the chair / clearly the difference /
of my body here / instead of there / is a promise / to never be /
neatened / by a threat / to threaten back / only with the flex / of my
back / & to offer / my body / one more time / than i should / so that
my children / know / when my blood / finally crisps / upon this
landscape / it will do so / in defiance / of a wind / that never offered /
to stop / carrying the cannon / sounds / the arch / the arching / the
gravity / of the fall

before the war begins the war begins

the nitrogen braids the burials / before the bottles of wine / can be placed upon the windowsill / america prefers to use / as target practice / & since peace is a hero / that almost exists / the glass will chase the glass / the rubble will chase the rubble / & only the blood will rise / high enough to be seen / by the meetings that inhabit the meetings / that have replaced the people / that replaced the people / that abstract the people / into numbers / & since winning / is losing / is winning / is as constantly almost as a hero / that emerges from death / as if that is the same thing / as living / as if any idea of war / could refuse to drip before the tide / takes our plasma as belonging / to an ocean that can / ever continue silently in this / context / we have been given / a howling / that does not fit / in our throats / that we have tried to shove / down the throats of others / & when they spit it back / at us / at america / we call that aggression / we call that the first volley / & when they decide it is best to choke on our gifts / to appease the directors / of this terrible scene / we consider that a selfish act / that they would die without / our help / without allowing us to emerge / as somehow righteous / that because they bought wine / they drank the wine with love / with others that love / that they wanted to remember / that wine by framing / the bottle amidst the whole world / we took that simple reflection / of light through a glass we did not make / or get a chance to empty / as a sign that only fire / could bring us closer / to the god we expected

neverwell #25

I have almost eight years
of sober thoughts
& all of them
curve my hips back
to the past where I was
a body in a basement
that refused to rise
because of a trauma
I could not think
to frame my mouth
around. That partial
guilt gives me what now?
All the names that are
tattooed on my body
have propped me up
for years, so maybe nobody
put me in that basement.
Maybe it was the safest
place to be a drunk?
I am the whole village fed
for weeks by this
temporary belief
& I confess, actual hunger
has started to braid me.

neverwell #37

I know how best
not to dream
at night. I know
the dust—no matter
how much sweep-
ing that I do—
remains in the air.
I live, necessarily,
without a picture
of the hole
behind my eyes.
I speak quietly
all the time.
I'm not supposed
to be thought of
in the morning.

neverwell #38

My births
have all
been steady.
It's the dying
I can't do
for shit.
It's the living
I can't apple.

neverwell #39

Most of my wanting
is lost in the translation
from Ohio to Ohia.

neverwell #80

Don't you think
that if I had
an agent I could
simplify this world
by having them
release one state-
ment about me,
my love of not
transcending
& then you all
could help me
stay here, sober
& safe forever?

neverwell #81

I wish I was alive
in a different way.

[native to a land free]

native to a land free
from plans we are still sleeping
in the buried gardens

of understanding the breath
this world does not come from
our lungs we are terribly

unjustified from mouth
to path the birds are bemused
we are the luxury

[what a delight for this]

what a delight for this
world to let go of loving
us back to combat this

looking into our own eyes
to decide if rivers
should keep their shallow shale lips

from kissing ours the puff
bond is always the weakest
the bloom paradox limps

[a raspberry cannot lie]

a raspberry cannot lie
in my mouth without the slight
fuzz seducing my tongue

into a violent roll
into my teeth i feel
no shame i never feel shame

the world is red enough
that i see the real problem
is only ever my mouth

[maybe having children]

maybe having children
was a mistake i can't stop
shaking when i think they

could be the last adults they
could kiss the first tide in
ohio i am thrilled they

are here now with me i
needed them but my needs are
bringing forth the ocean

Replacing the Monument #58

There is no soft
repair.

Emily as the Community Pool When it Rains

There are reasons
the tide waits
for the storm.

There are reasons
why I am the only one
on the lounge chair

when Emily gets going.
I know the lightning
goes looking.

I so badly want
to be found by her
that any

of summer's metaphors
will do. Besides
a lifeguard gets chased

& Emily
& I, we can
really have some fun.

Emily as I Prepare the Meal-Kit Pork Carnitas Bowl

There is an owl
that visits the dying
tree that fell

onto our backyard
shed. It arrives
as a blessing

I assume. I see it
through the kitchen
window sometimes.

I've set off
the smoke alarm
while I watch it

in tears from jalapeño
& the crushing idea
that this world

is a burnt place now.
There are still tools
in that shed.

I don't want to touch
metal anymore.
I've offered my eyes

to that owl,
but I'm to see all
of this

& to keep feeding
the children.
Freedom requires
many witnesses.

Emily as I Prepare the Meal-Kit Cheesy Chicken & Pepper Quesadilla

There are a lot of ships
& not a lot of ocean
in a marriage.

We cannot deny
there is water just because
nobody went anywhere

today. We taste salt
without swimming
all the time.

Emily as I Prepare the Meal-Kit Hoisin Pork Sloppy Joes

I want the painkillers our dog is taking.
I want a new soul out of nothing.
Emily says

this meal comes with potato buns.
I want potato buns.
I want days that are more than just was.

I want the clutching of my children
during a pandemic to mean I love them
enough to stay sober.

I want a lung to stay a lung.
I want the mosquitos that track me
from the creek bed to take the blood they need.

I want the word I use
to be more than just coffin slang. I want a meal
to once again be more than a eulogy of sorts.

Emily as We Bring Ourselves to the Creek
for Bianca Stone

Not all ferocity
is gothic, but we bring

our favorite paintings
to the edge

of the light
& undeniable force

of a casual water
that dies all the time,

but refuses to die
without our witness.

How much
of a fairy tale is the oil

that holds on
to the canvasses

we offer fifty yards from
the land we own?

How much does it matter
that we use four hands

to drown the art
we've brought? That is

such a limited question.
Besides, we re-hang it all.

Emily as the Thunder Comes

Let's say the death threats
are not written
by cowards this time

& Ohio has finally decided
to return me
to the Kokosing. How much

lightning will it take
for the rest of the country
to see she is the most beautiful

widow? A sunflower
is always a sunflower.
My body's final coloring

won't change the fact
that at midnight you can see
Emily amidst any storm.

Emily as a Single Discovery

The tenth tattoo
is an ink spot
among other ink spots.

I was once buried in

a herd of black horses.
I was never alone
amidst their dark hair.

Now, I teach chants

to chairs most of the time.
There is so much hard
matter in my life.

There is one song. Do
not follow me past
the woods of this poem.

Emily as We Salvage the Spill

Each hair she leaves behind
is a gallon of coffee
& since I gave up

on the usefulness of water
I maintain our dedication
with dry towels.

It all gets pretty raw here.
We rely on the byproduct
of life to move us forward.

I slide in reality. I am
an easy target. It's Emily
that sloshes

so radically against
the alleys of a swallowable
life. What tide?

Allow me to prove
the theory of our loving mess
by dragging you through it.

Emily as a Plum Flower

Either way, the horse
will be approaching
from the black river

with all those teeth
& no patience. The end
is the end. I choose

to be found with any part
of her bloom in my mouth.
I will not fumble

her gift in an attempt to
position myself separately from
my lack of understanding.

Emily as a Tré Burt Song

I drew a portrait of Emily
in water I was not holding.
It seemed like enough for her.

It was not enough for her.
I carved her likeness in the ice
of a landmass that was headed

south. That made her cry.
I made soup for her when she
was not hungry. From the couch,

she said it smelled delicious,
but she never ate any of it. I am
nothing in the context of time,

& Emily is nothing in the con-
text of time. I've never cared
about time. It's not Emily.

Emily as Tea

There is a spirit, a throb,
a question

& another question
& a reason why

my throat bobs
up

& down,
like acceptance

is an answer
that needs repetition,

that needs convincing
& a good swim

through all doubt.
I skid into

& out of this world
all the time.

When you find me
standing up,

it's because I believe
on that day

I will taste Emily,
the steam of her,

& that keeps
my airways open.

Emily as a Primary Function

I neither love
nor take
care of Emily.

I end
the West
for her.

I bring
her oceans.
I am devoted

to the action
of her knives.
I am cut

when she
needs me
to be cut.

Her neck
pulses
& I exist.

She closes
her eyes
& I can't.

translating intimacy in march

let us not suppose
that some weather
will bury

our bodies
before the people
that storm

our hearts
are willing to lash us
to the opposite

of their desires
we cannot pinch
the present

between the thighs
of an alarm
that is always silent

winter with its sharp fingers

for Alina Stefanescu

sparrow-mouthed from where
the cedar chips cannot warm
& all of the fifteenth days pass

without the violence, the must
& the must have, the purple
hope of defiance, the whole

of nature, which reaches past
the spasms of winter, which
gives the faithful feeling

an observation podium,
a reality that does not ask
the astonishing to be evidence

of anything, i call, i call to say
i am lost in weather like this,
in this weathering world

& you, you say you can see me
underneath not much more
than a small fit of berries

An Ode to the Line-drives as They Curl to Drop Thirty Feet Beyond the Second Baseman Over & Over Again in My Dreams

You can tell me
it's the same
as moving a chair

from one corner
of my mind to another,
but I only know

how to peg a fastball
on the inside black
while I'm looking

for a pitch away.
My hands hold a flood
for the weak spot

in the riverbank.
It doesn't matter
that I don't hit it flush,

I round first
without a catch
in my knees.

The water is smooth
in my quick-twitch
dreams.

I wait months for it
to roll me bare
into the crop

of my youth. I am
still the bloom when
I describe the bloom.

As I Grew Up Surrounded by James Wright's Suicidally-Beautiful Football Players

We all lose
the treasure
as we lose sight

of what stands out
as treasure
in the flat places

of Ohio, where
Wright had us
all watching

the old men
as they watched
the young men

& those rafted
dreams we all held
or dropped

dramatically on
& off the field,
our knees refusing

each generation's
request. It wasn't
even much

of a cheer. I didn't
know, we would all
so deeply consider

suicide by the time
we were forty.
Good lord, only

the silence cared
enough to follow us.
Our bodies, they

became bodies.

An Easy Dinner

Work or act, we drop our minds
into sustaining this momentum, we
decide in the moment what

will keep the five of us from being
overtaken by the light, by the wind,
by the end of the day when we don't

care so much about labor's gnawing
or life's thrusting panic. The children
all want to order pizza again.

We all want to order pizza again,
but there's broccoli left over
& some rice, two-thirds

of a chicken breast. The oldest
child makes her own dinner
with fresh food because she can.

The middle child asks for dessert.
The youngest remembers the mac
& cheese her Monday caregiver

made for her. It's a victory
that there's a little extra shredded
in the store's default cheese bag

so we can sprinkle a bit of it
on top of the macaroni to make it
new again in a way the youngest

child doesn't want. My partner
uses avocado oil to heat a veggie
burger. I start doing the dishes
while the microwave counts down
to what noise? New plates
arrive. I eat my gifts. It's bedtime.

Domestic Mannerism

I hung the apple
& the lemon
from my throat

one obscenely bright morning
to force attention
to the bloom that used to

arrive outside of our house
& each of the children
that caught the new colors

beneath my beard
asked me
about the extreme world

that locked our doors.
I couldn't think to frame
my mouth

around the words
of the garden,
so I sparrow-lipped

the un-teaching lessons
of our modern pains
& they let me talk

until they grew hungry
enough to snatch the fruit
with all six hands.

It was pleasant, to be plucked
& still alive. I'll never forget
how their stunted wandering
felt different that day.
They almost traveled
with that skin in their teeth.

instead of watching the presidential debate i finally listen to the taylor swift album *folklore*

for Emily Caldwell

it's not that i don't want to witness the conflagration
of america's obscene caste system while they shuffle
the deck of ugliness as if time as motion can justify the energy
& death they so lovingly kitsch to separate the camps
of our nation — i know one of those men has asked
for my death i know one of those men doesn't care if i die —
i just wanted to keep the lights off in my house while
my children slept as believers in the history of beauty
& before there was another attempt to scorch the hair
from the top of my head i leaned into the popular intimacy
as soft & valuable as it can be —
to learn the new words without an allegorical interpretation
to learn the shining fibers we can use to make cozy
sweaters in this day where there is hope in the lower
registers where the traditional white devils are blind
we don't need the nose nor the mouth of this reality
we just need a skin that can breathe through every season
we just need to be free enough for the breeze to find us

i do not ask how to love without a ceiling i do not ask how to drown without a river i do not ask how to hear the paper bells

written for Zeina Hashem Beck, after the explosion at the port in the city of Beirut

no nation wants its people
to outlive it
even if we lived in the song cave

gave that depth a new name
the opening to all that splendid black
would not allow us to leave it

without first touching our bones
now now now i am told
that the absence of hands can crater a home

that not looking for the spark
in a world on fire pierces the air
into witness

burns more beds than monsters
& makes us all ghost children
that must carry dead children towards

the hyphens that cannot create a new body
that cannot silent the beating
our heart takes

that blasts open fate's haughty smile
& leaves our jaws without a joy that
can nightsong in earnest

or dream about with a full mouth
of our city's plated history
this steam this smoke

that is still rising today
will want to loosen the fire
from the ashes

& all we can do
without a vibrating farewell
to these terrible men that only taste meat

& can only call their ships toys
& their people candles to be lit in their name
& celebrate that a corpse

is not jobless because it fulfills the need
to be a dead thing
is hope that when the poets choose

to become sharp stars
they are not gentle when they blanket us
that their words can smother

& wound
the escaping limits of the time this world
decided it didn't belong here

temple piece #1

all art is gothic art if you believe
the lake is on fire for other reasons
then probably this place is holy

temple piece #10

mouth the word *cinnamon* when any person
tells you they have spoken to the tumbleweed
of god if they don't lick their lips they're lying

temple piece #13

smother the inelegance with more inelegance trip those betting
on the moon get caught up in the haphazard layering of your own
dripping temples swim the lake of it you cowards dive dive dive

temple piece #27

it's a foot or it's birdseed something has to bang
into the cloth of those narrow nouns something
has to force us past this okay god okay narrative

cravings #11
For Tommye Blount

every burn turns blue
if you refuse to look at it
if you refuse to widespread
the sentiment that the fire
was started in error

that the scarring on my skin
should matter to you
if i am wearing a shirt
on the back porch of this
sober epoch this freedom

from the bubbles their pop
to body again in the echo
of the art that is too often
called the ashes of just what
did you think a body was

horror theory #8

sure sure sure cool
modernity is hollow
ancient was careless

all of the religions
are so terribly beautiful
& violently certain

if i leave my body here
it will harden
it will soften

it will be cleaned
by strangers
without imagination

the only achievements
are disobedience
& close-up magic

trust the fantasia
you can read in the light
you can read in the dark

i'm gonna stand up now (with this love)
for my daughter, isabelle

there is a metaphysics to love there is also an orange peel that will never
be thrown away that will never be framed as art that will rot in a jar and
in the essential memory of when our oldest daughter let her hands
become spent candles as we told her there would be another baby that
stopped mid-peel on her snack to hold her own heart as a gift for her
unborn sister and when i went to trash the forgotten fruit i could not
think to let it escape forever so i wiped clean a jar that had been filled
with buttons so that it could allow the mold to grow safely away from the
corner of my eye where i always prefer to hide the realistic beauty of
fatherhood those incidents that are just compassion sped up to fit into a
wednesday there there there the color fades with inaction but the triumph
of their hearts remains in motion grows into a penicillin for my own
weaknesses fogs a jar without new air makes the art i spend my time
circling to erase or deceiving into stanzas worth far less than the table i
washed to display the jar with orange peel on my oldest daughter's
eleventh birthday as she enters the kitchen to eat again to turn on and off
the lights around me to ask me what i am working on so i can tell her
nothing important that this poem is nothing important let it be canon i
love my children more than i will ever love poetry let it be canon this
poem any of my poems could have ended better but one of my children
has inevitably said my name out loud and i have abandoned the poem the
same way i will abandon it now

The Museum Is Free on Sundays

Woozy in the blue breeze,

I found the bastard's conduit
in the sponsorship

& the naming
of the sponsorship
after capitalism's dead wife.

Look! The tethers have
all been cut
& the rope-makers
have decided to frame

the performance
while they drown us in
oceans of rope. The rupture
must, but I refuse to trade
one day for six. That shit has

only ever given us thresholds
& doors & gods
& slavery. We sail only
because there is wind
& a moon. We create thickness
as a dance to encourage

a proper rubbing. If fire comes,
don't trap it in a building.
Let it burn like a beast
with no plan. I am only
for the art that routes us
through their melting fat.
I am only for the naming

that removes the distance
between the rabbit's breath
& the rabbit's flight. Follow
me to the fields. The real
fuckery is done hiding

& it's free & free & free
& free & free & free & free.

Acknowledgments

Adirondack Review – bone requires bone #46; bone requires bone #47

After the Pause – Replacing the Monument #58

Another Chicago Magazine – We Are Arrows #88; with an empathy so fatal #21

Arkana – War Commentary #51

Banyan Review – winter with its sharp fingers

Bear Review – Emily as a Plum Flower

The Bees Are Dead – Trump as a Fire Without Light #86

Blueline – Emily as the Length of a Fox

Borderlands – Nude Male with Echo #197

Chattahoochee Review – Firework Over the Retention Pond #4

Cimarron – The Field Party #1

Colorado Review – Emily as a Primary Function; Emily as Tea

Cortland Review – neverwell #25

Cotton Xenomorph – Emily as the Thunder Comes

Dalhousie Review – Emily as I Hold Three of Her Shoes; Unfinished Murder Ballad: The Only Dedicated Cowboy in Columbus, Ohio Objects to the Price of His Black Coffee

DIAGRAM – Emily as Where We Sigh

Dream Pop – Emily as the Community Pool When it Rains

Emerge – Firework Over the Retention Pond #1

The Finger – A Letter to Auguste Rodin, Explaining the Bombing of the Thinker

Fissure – Trump as a Fire Without Light #12

Five South – Emily as I Prepare the Meal-kit Pork Carnitas Bowl

Flypaper – Utica, Ohio

Former People – A Damaged Thinker #16

Fourteen Hills – Unfinished Murder Ballads: The Girl Was a Raspberry

Fredericksburg Literary Review – A Damaged Thinker #20

Guesthouse – Emiy as a Song Written by Tré Burt

Glass: before the war begins the war begins; i do not ask how to love without a ceiling i do not ask how to drown without a river i do not ask how to hear the paper bells; red milk

Grasslimb – Nude Male with Echo #55

Great Lakes Review – neverwell #37; neverwell #38; neverwell #39

Grist – Emily as a Leveling of Ground

Hawaii Pacific Review – Huckleberry Pie

Hotel Amerika – Emily as She Dropped the Lantern at My Feet

Inflectionist Review – Nude Male with Echo #1

Jet Fuel – Emily as the Audacity of the Red Egg, Unfinished Murder Ballad: The Sea Naked

Juked – Ohio #5

Lickety-split – translating intimacy in march

Little Rose – with an empathy so fatal #7

Lost Coast – Nude Male with Echo #257

Louisville Review – We Did Our Best to Breathe Into It

Many Nice Donkeys – Emily as I Prepare the Meal-Kit Cheesy Chicken & Pepper Quesadilla

Mascara Review – Trump as Fire Without Light #340

The Maynard – Trump as a Fire Without Light #665

Meadow – Nude Male with Echo #319

Menacing Hedge – We Are Arrows #209

Minetta Review – Ode to the Corner of the Drug House Down the Gravel Road off the Two-Lane Highway #60

Moon City – "What the Fuck Are You Telling Me?"

NōD – i'm gonna stand up now (with this love)

North American Review – Emily as We Salvage the Spill; if there is a river #55

North Dakota Review – The Tension Between the Concrete and the Ethereal

One – Nude Male with Echo #70

OxMag – How Vital Sport?

Parcel – The Moon is Too Big to Be the Moon; Not a Leaf, Falls Like a Leaf

Pank – layering

Parentheses Journal – Emily as We Bring Ourselves to the Creek

Petrichor – with an empathy so fatal #56

Pine Hills Review – Sweet Wolf #1

Posit – All the Birds Are Leaving #79

Puerto del Sol – Trump as a Fire Without Light #415; Trump as a Fire Without Light #416; Trump as a Fire Without Light #417

Qua – Emily as a Puma Crosses

Rabble Review – neverwell #80; neverwell #81

Really System – Emily as a Smile Would Have Ruined the Picture

Rise Up Review – [those junk plums]

Rogue Agent – Nude Male with Echo #244; Trump as a Fire Without Light #140; with an empathy so fatal #52

Shantih – blue and blue and blue #63

Slag Review – I Have No Intention of Burying My Body #52

Smoking Glue Gun – We Are Arrows #2

Spoon River Poetry – All the Birds Are Leaving #60

Stirring – We Are Arrows #26

Sundog Lit – Emily as Measureless

Sweet Literary – Emily as I Prepare the Meal-Kit Hoisin Pork Sloppy Joes

Sweet Tree – if there is a river #28

Thrush – blue and blue and blue #3; Emily as Our Lust is a Common Lust

Tuck Magazine – Trump as a Fire Without Light #115

Twykenham Notes – Emily as a Book of Endings

Whale Road Review – [you *might choose to read these poems*]
*Words & Sports Quarterly – An Ode to the Line-drives as They Curl to Drop
Thirty Feet Beyond the Second Baseman Over & Over Again in My Dreams; As I
Grew Up Surrounded by James Wright's Suicidally-Beautiful Football Players*
Umbrella Factory – We Are Arrows #8
Unbroken – Unfinished Murder Ballad: Caribou
Uptown 1 – Nude Male with Echo #299
Variety Pack – Emily as a Single Discovery
Weber: The Contemporary West – All the Birds Are Leaving #64
Wick Poetry Center – the wind has never cared
Yesmassee – blue and blue and blue #133; blue and blue and blue #134
Yes Poetry – america chose to drown in the desert
Ygdrasil – When Men Talk About Sam Cooke
Zaira – Unfinished Murder Ballad: The Walls Slid Back Down, Joining
Zaum – Emily as a Pious Crowd & a Rabbit
Zombie Logic – Sweet Wolf #13
Zoomoozophone Review – blue and blue and blue #6

Darren C. Demaree is the author of twenty-four full-length poetry collections, most recently "Now Flourish Northern Cardinal (Selected Poems 2005-2025)", (Small Harbor Publishing, November 2025). He is the recipient of an Ohio Arts Council Individual Excellence Award, the Louise Bogan Award from Trio House Press, and the Nancy Dew Taylor Award from Emrys Journal.

About Small Harbor Publishing

Small Harbor Publishing is a 501c3 nonprofit organization. Our goal is to publish unique and diverse voices. We are a feminist press, and we are committed to diversity and inclusion. We strive to bring new voices to a devoted and expanding readership.

Small Harbor Publishing began in 2018 with the first issue of *Harbor Review*. The magazine is an online space where poetry and art converse. *Harbor Review* quickly grew and now publishes reviews and runs multiple micro chapbook competitions, including the Washburn Prize and the Editor's Prize.

In July 2020, Small Harbor Publishing was officially incorporated and began Harbor Editions. Harbor Editions accepts submissions through a chapbook open reading period, a hybrid chapbook open reading period, the Marginalia Series, and the Laureate Prize.

In 2023, Harbor Anthologies began with a mission to promote texts that explore social justice issues and highlight marginalized writers.

If you would like to support Small Harbor Publishing, visit our "About" page at: smallharborpublishing.com/about.

www.ingramcontent.com/pod-product-compliance
Lightning Source LLC
Chambersburg PA
CBHW020201090426
42734CB00008B/904